# OPEN SECRET

Photograph by Bob Laramie, courtesy of the *Holyoke Transcript-Telegram*.

# Open Secret

COLIN WAY REID

Drawings by Carol Blakney

COLIN SMYTHE
Gerrards Cross, 1986

Copyright © 1986 by B. L. Reid
First published in 1986 by Colin Smythe Limited
Gerrards Cross, Buckinghamshire


**British Library Cataloguing in Publication Data**

Reid, Colin Way
Open secret.
I. Title
811'.54   PS3568.E476/

ISBN 0—86140—240—5

Produced in Great Britain
Set by Grove Graphics, Tring, Herts,
and printed and bound by Billing & Sons Ltd.,
Worcester

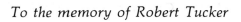

*To the memory of Robert Tucker*

# Contents

## Chinese Essay

The light plum sky
is veined with branches
and the laurels darkening
curl in the cold,
trembling like dogs.

It is the season
of unchange
and I wait to find
a flicker
in the trees.

Soon, surely,
down the road
will come a word
of summer
in the sound
of water on the hill.

Blue snow and laurels,
lights returning up
and into dark,
take with you
this letter
down the night of bells.

## Three Cranes

At dusk the world they live in seems all white
except the black that floats them in the sky,
holding them like long shapes in a shadow-
box: pale shadows, ghosts in frozen light,
they bring the snow. The Chinese cranes can fly
out of the iris and the grass below
into the northern winter like three words,
a storm of wings, an eddy in the dust
of icy sky. The chaste and knowing birds
unfold the weather in a molt of pride,
a coming down of angels in a tide,
a flickering of feathers in the deep
above, before, inside: the seasons trust
the three cranes and the flakes of snow they sweep.

## Eros*

So glittering on black you gold
from leaf to flower climbing draw
the present point cast in the old
design. Your law

decided at the tip to catch
has flickered almost out of art.
On wings, in shadows quick you snatch
a timeless arrow for your heart,

advancing limberly in string
bend bow to carry home intent:
yet you, caught on the vase's ring,
will never more than get bow bent.

No verb, you noun who seem to act;
so energetic yet so still
your purpose; in your face the fact
indomitable of your will.


*From a gold-painted Lekythos.

## Temenos*

A shadow is the shape behind,
inside the stone. They come from deep,
these likenesses of our bright kind,
as if we find them in our sleep.

Under the skin of deities
we lose ourselves in virgin stone.
The silence the old sculptor frees
is not the gods'. It is our own.

We wonder at the absent face
worn by these gentlefolk who seem
to loiter godly out of place
within the temenos of dream.

Beyond the surface, past the light
thin layer of the easy real,
we need to use the second sight.
Divinity is what we feel.


*A sacred precinct. After sculptures from the East Frieze of the
Parthenon, in the British Museum, London.

# Hypnos*

Onewinged Sleep, you hover on a dream
that has forgotten your bronze head. You sigh.
And that is you, the exhalation pure
as all forgetting on the edging seam
of day and night, earth and teeming sky
with gods or men translated. Subtle, sure,
you sidle in our veins despite the shape
you've fallen into, or perhaps without.
You are a drug of power and of grace.
Your quiet sounds the depth of our escape,
Hypnos, spiriting invisibly—lights out!—
you find your way and we forget your face
as, silently and in a mood of prayer,
we are led downward into darker air.

*The sculpture referred to is the head of Hypnos in the British
Museum.

## The Evangelist Matthew*

The angel hovers dark behind,
filling St. Matthew with the light
he must remember if his mind
will carry through his hand real sight,

deliver to the page designed
the vision in whose quiet flight
the angel hovers dark behind,
filling St. Matthew with the light.

In this creation he can find
the truth neither in black nor white,
a chiaroscuro, day in night
as seen and unseen come combined:
the angel hovers dark behind.


*After the painting of that name by Rembrandt, in the
Louvre, Paris.

## Rembrandt's Tobit

a poem in eight parts based on
Rembrandt's depictions of scenes from
the Book of Tobit
in the Apocrypha

## 1  Why*

He woke up in the morning blind.
A swallow shat in his old eyes
as he lay sleeping in his mind.
He almost lost that too before
he found his way in his own door
and sat, sure that he could not rise.

Between the windows and the fire
he waited in an absent light
for his slow flicker to expire
and for Tobias to return.
And Anna watched him smoke and burn,
spinning their thread into the night.

It seems the purpose of the son
to find the fish (surprising key)
and with its gall get the work done;
to touch the old man and make sure
the love in and behind the cure
is strong enough to make him see.

*After the drawing *Tobit Asleep*, in the Museum Boymans-van
Beuningen, Rotterdam.

## 2   The Wheel*

Tobit would listen to her spin.
The click and whir, and her own hum
mixed with the wheel's, made sense to him.
And she would look out on the town
to tell him who went up and down.
The thread she spun would twist and come

fine, strong, the way he liked to feel
its purpose tense between his hands.
It gave him light, almost, the wheel.
He could imagine what she said
and give up wishing to be dead.
Tobias perhaps understands,

taking his worries to the loft
and wondering what he will do.
The slow fire with its crackle soft
speaks crumbling in his sleepy eyes.
Anna stays by it till it dies.
The story spins them swift and true.


*A composite of several depictions and imagination.

## 3  The Three of Them*

Arrested, Tobit clasps his hands.
Outside in some far land of light,
he knows, Tobias understands,
sure as the spinning wheel, what fire
draws them together, what desire
a son and father need to fight

the distance they require between:
and Tobit's own remembered road
spins out behind. What do they mean
to one another, these three fates?
Rembrandt in this case understates
how each, connected, shifts his load:

how Anna, spinning, waits in work
while her son, with the angel's aid,
cuts bravely, slowly, through the murk
that clouds his father's strong belief
into his own wife's house of grief,
and home. Three threads, a single braid.

*After the painting *Tobit and Anna Waiting*, in the Museum
van der Vorm, Rotterdam.

## 4   The Fish*

Surprise! A magic fish takes shape
and leaps and snaps. Tobias shrinks.
The angel from his own escape
looks calmly on the nasty sign
and hands his friend a hook and line
(perhaps). The scene God makes and thinks

complete with cow and farmers deep
in view, cliffs rising fatal, sheer
above the mysteries that sleep
and wake in these slow distant trees:
this is the real scene Rembrandt sees
around Tobias' comic fear.

The River Tigris does not know
the story it has spawned and fed.
All miracles must somewhere grow
in the creator's fictive mind
as paths and rivers shift and wind.
Tobias went where he was led.


*After the drawing *Tobias Frightened by the Fish*, in the
Albertina, Vienna.

## 5   Return*

There's something funny. Raphael
may not really be there at all.
But some guardian—who can tell?—
distracts Tobias on,
brings him the hope he finds in dawn
and leads him into night's long fall.

So very funny. Through those wings
some Rembrandt does not care to look.
Can Sarah see—as she bumps, sings
a donkeyriding marriage song—
certain as she rides along,
Tobias (as they cross the brook)

is her man? Tobias smiles.
This man with odd wings is sure.
This man lifts and reconciles
him to Fate, the journey home.
He does not return alone
but happily carries the cure.


*After the drawing *The Return of Tobias and Sarah*, in a
private collection, Newbury, Berkshire.

## 6  Welcome*

The blind man in his ringing cave
gropes deeply for the hidden word
heard from the comfort of the grave.
So unfamiliar, gone so long.
The nearness of the spoken song
moves Tobit to the voice he heard.

The moment wavers at this crux,
Tobit still feeling for the door,
his trouble gathering from flux
to meet the embodiment of joy
in his miraculous dark boy.
Now as the heart of his slow sore

comes open in his hand and face,
he needs. That is the meaning here.
He does not reach for light or grace
but only for his only son;
and only when the way is won
will he look back and see it clear.

*After the etching *Tobit Moving to Welcome his Son.*

## 7  Surgery*

The tense conjunction and its poise,
a magic distillate in time,
lives in that depth beyond the noise
of children playing in the sun.
Tobias has his growing done.
He bends now in his able prime,

the power gathered in his deft
and loving hands to sting the sight
back in those eyes. The warp and weft
of Tobit's memory will be
lit in the new way he can see.
Already something's coming bright:

long in that deep and lonely maze
with Anna's voice, with no dog's bark,
he nears the threshold of real days
again and feels the strange old sense
of light and colour in suspense
waking in his frustrated dark.


*After the painting *Tobias Healing Tobit's Blindness,* in the
Staats-galerie, Stuttgart.

## 8   Departure*

See how the angel lifts, and takes
a backward look at Sarah, leaves
with sudden glory. Silence breaks:
we hear the rush of Rembrandt's sound
dashing in his ears. On the ground
a family of faith conceives

power. And the angel knows
as they come to know him, *now*.
Raphael, companion, *goes*;
and following him with her eyes,
Sarah clasps hands; Tobit falls. Wise?
Who is wise? All wonder. How

does a winged angel look? Look!
Miracle! It was all real.
I vanish. See? Here in my book
you may keep my image, friend:
see, Tobias, how we end
and what divine wings we conceal.

*After the painting *The Angel Departs*, in the Louvre, Paris.

## After William Blake

I    Frontispiece, *Songs of Innocence*

The piper holds a reeded pipe,
An oboe with a voice as ripe
As yonder cloud, which holds the child
Who spreads his arms as if beguiled
And calms the sheep, and calls the tune
From Blake's self figure, piping June.
The sheep stretch far across the glade;
The man and boy are by wind made;
The trees stretch up their nether hands;
The cloud puffs east, and music stands.

II    Title Page, *Songs of Innocence*

The tree of innocence, entwined
With an encircling, rising vine,
Is partial, in itself and in
Its attitude; it stretches wide
And takes the universe to ride.

The nurse or mother in the chair
Holds out the book and breathes the air
Of innocence; its rhyming line
Spreads out before the little folk,
Those acorns of a simple oak.

The sky is full of flying men:
Babe in the O, angel in N,
And one behatted trumpeter
Leaning into the graceful I —
Perhaps Blake's truth in his own eye.

One more figure, then pass to birds
Who fly among the floating words
And leave the fruit to grow full ripe.
Lastly, crucially, the time:
Seventeen hundred and eighty-nine.

III   'Infant Joy', *Songs of Innocence*

Joy rests in something like a flower,
A wild plant of green, blue and power.
Sweet joy rests in its mother's arms,
An angel blesses child with charms:
'Sweet joy befall thee'; and a plant,
That miracle, seems but to want
the babe to rest in its suspense;
Like a cloud's but far far more dense.

IV   Title page, *Songs of Experience*

Once when he 'stain'd the water clear',
Blake wrote a song and spread a bier.
On the bier he laid an ancient pair
And showed the daughters weeping there.
Now if experience is sight
There must be some who'd paint this night;
But Blake has put it in clear day,
To show that death is worse this way.

V  'The Tyger' and 'The Sick Rose',
   *Songs of Experience*

The tyger blazoned on the page
Is wrought with fervour and with rage.
The rainbow of his coat becomes
The rainbow on the page, the poem's.
His fearful symmetry is gross
And shining in green, yellow, rose.

The rose is sick and full of worm;
It scrapes the ground and blows its germ
Out, as it dies, upon the world,
While spirits lie in branches furled.
These bend their heads and mourn their friend's
Soon end; her joy to sadness wends.

O Blake! You piper in sheer sun!
Your life is past, your work is done;
But of the artists whom we see,
None lifts his wand and pipe like thee.

## Adirondack Guide*

He balancing waits for the waver's break
in the shape of a rose or a rainbow,
watching his life (maybe) rise in the lake

where the shadows of memory flit and fake.
Thoughts can rise up: *That damn fish is slow.*
He balancing waits for the waver's break

to plunge him in deep, deeper down; to take
one last breath home to the world below,
watching his life (maybe) rise in the lake

to meet him, his friends reaching upward shake
loose of the dark and embrace him. So
he balancing waits for the waver's break.

The slivers of gold, blue, vermilion flake
above the fascinating clear. *What, no?*—
watching his life (maybe) rise in the lake

he forgets the fish in his own wide wake
and would turn if he could, but forgets to go:
he balancing waits for the waver's break,
watching his life (maybe) rise in the lake.


*After the watercolour of that name by Winslow Homer, in the
Museum of Fine Arts, Boston.

## Playing a Fish*

*For my mother*

Ghosts on twilit lake. This painting
plays me like a fish on hook and line.
It has me by the tongue. It takes my mind.
I speak in jerks. The fisherman hears fainting
silent words and pulls again. Here in the lake
that sunlight has searched through I die slow as
the evening dies, mottled pink and blue. We pass
into a painted world for someone's sake.

That someone is the watcher who can show
his sketching mind: Winslow Homer, a ghost
of sorts himself, takes his place in this vast
little sunset and outside. We watch him row
his hidden self in the lake where he is lost
and paint himself into the water's past.

*On the painting of the same name by Winslow Homer at the Clark
Institute in Williamstown, Massachusetts.

# The Sleeping Gypsy

*For Dargan Jones*

The depth of colour in invented night
sleeps waking in the witness and the scene.
The lion carries all in his weird sight;
he is the hairy monolith of dream.

Motion has found its lyric end in rest.
The rainbow gathered at the waist flows on
into the desert moonlight; and the guest,
the beast-in-waiting, breathes the pause from song.

The Gypsy has no meat for the cat to steal,
holds only her stick, her way to begin;
the lion is there to make a fancy real
as pale dunes, a moon and a mandolin.


*On the painting of that name by Henri Rousseau in the Museum of
Modern Art in New York.

## Degas' Horses*

Here Degas' horses pace
faint in sunlight,
shadowdeep. The track
like some sky needs
their dance, reflecting
and absorbing slow the prance
and skitter, slant like knife
of shine, their long noon
freed to slip from step
to highstep, conjure
grace.

*After the painting *At the Race Course*, in the Louvre,
Paris.

## The Snake Charmer*

Jungle, where the desert kept
her secret while the Gypsy slept;
tune, and unimaginably
charm, seduction, pagan grace:
eyes in a dark undertree
byariver inaface,
deity's unquestioned place:
Rousseau makes invulnerable—
music? No. But almost. Hear

as the flute slips up the scale
of the snakes who come to listen
to the river's slap and glisten,
with the innocence of trance
give up all and leave no trail
in coming. So did that Gypsy sister
walk from the realm of mere romance
into the riskier world of dream
and as reward left no trace,
inventing her own timeless place. So
this mistress can redeem
the intimate exotic world
that gathers, perched and rooted, curled
about her most essential song.
And every hearer will belong.

*After the painting of that name by Henri Rousseau, in the Louvre, Paris.

40

## The Three Musicians

Instant, shiver. Skip
in my vein with the catch of
jazz.
       Blithe undertakers,
flicker. Birdlike. Perched
in quick costume,
edge inside me.
                Eyes cut in faces
open silence. That's where I find you
talking music, what in this rhythm
sidles deeper, sifting the moment like
a feather sinking into the distance
brightly.

## May Day*

That colour should become so clear,
shadow suggest so much of sun
and celebration disappear
the way this May Day would have done,

all seem to carry silence home,
that silence that enraptures paint
come brightly and to each alone,
silence that admits a faint

but rising decibel in chime
of voices spinning streamers, song;
a dance: concatenation: time
in one of those scenes that belong

to ideal memory or dream;
and red and yellow, pink and blue
surrender to the coming green
the breath come preternaturally through

loving open eyes and brush
into our lungs, into our minds;
that daylight should at last lift, flush
into a flourish that unwinds

like pennants, ribbons in the breeze
to float like children in the grass,
in particoloured reveries
to revel in the time they pass.


*After the watercolour *May Day, Central Park* by Maurice
Prendergast, in the Cleveland Museum of Art.

## Still Life: Le Jour*

Ring, guitar, and make the day
jumble itself out of jump:
always, such a composite,
things in falling into fit . . .
such a breakfast, pitcher, knife,
elements of where we are,
apples, glass, sunlight, guitar:
music in the hang of still
still still life.

Paris, and it's '29
unsettling into design
with the cubist breath of shape:
what a marvelous escape!
And we cannot rearrange
the angles of this new repose
waking with a paper angel
folded sensually on the table . . .
I suppose he read it when,
sometime after ten, the clock
reclaimed Georges Braque.

Thank you for this music, master,
for this light:
for the veering colour green
your sunsight refracted blackly.
Whang upon your instrument.
Throw the pipe away and cut
into an apple as big as the sun:
while you're up there having fun
drink for us a glass as pure
as the joy of this, Le Jour.

*After the painting of that name by Georges Braque, in the
National Gallery, Washington.

## In Pollaiuolo's Eye*

Daphne takes green branching leave
and already fast in bark,
distant, intimate, can mark
time with a last almost smile,
turn as if reluctant while
holding her, he loses,
clings—she footloose on laurel wings
rising in her rootedness
toward his bereaved sublime.

Her riverfather can refract
the classic valley's trees and sky,
careless, clear, forgetting, so
that in Pollaiuolo's eye
we harbour a perspective, reach
back into mountains' height
with this second's second sight,
trace the current to the spring
and find in its eternal tense
what Pollaiuolo follows, like Apollo
hunts: the lovely apparition, sad,
we carry in our antique sense
and colour with the shades of change.
No myth more sweetly is more strange.

As their eyes in parting meet,
her leg, leftover, mocks his chase
with loving, accidental grace:
he so desperately flesh
and she triumphant in the fresh
foreknowledge of her torture's end
pause, this momentary couple, speed
implicit in his ribbands; stream,
dream of flight and flight of dream.
In the quiet catch of paint
the story at its cruel turn
comes home to our weird hearts like wine,
lingers, something silent, fine.

*After the painting *Apollo and Daphne* by Antonio Pollaiuolo,
in the National Gallery, London.

## An Early Daphne

The sun falls off the edge of Daphne's wood
and leaves his children silent in her eye.
The mountains rumpling round her in a hood
of leafy weaving hide her from the sky.

For she sees danger in the warning clouds
that hold the day's last sun: a rape by day,
a sudden light upon her. She seeks shrouds
of hemlock branches and a darkened way.

Moon slips into the suspense of power.
The light is mild, yet Daphne sits in fear.
The beech wood shadows round her in that hour
when only owls make love, and doves, and deer.

## Daphne After

In the absence of a heart grown
stemwise, silent, slow Daphne drinks
unremembering and unknown,
in the manner of a laurel thinks

in branches, sometimes blossoms. Real
forgetting is her secret, long
detachment, no split sense to heal.
Only sentiment and song

remember how she suffered, ran
in terror, turning tree, and past
to present. Where the myth began,
the laurel is the light's at last.

## Pygmalion

My ivory lady, come and see
stone butterflies, cold cowries wake
into the life you take from me:
gifts, God knows, in a breath divined
to blossom in your absent mind.
My darling, my idea, break

and dangle in a web of thought,
conceiving, loving, giving birth:
Child! Form in whose slow stone I sought
the only woman I could reach,
do we not wonder, each in each?
We spring from the same abstract earth.

We suffer from one silence. Art,
supposed to answer, seems to smile,
drawing the chisel to the heart
and guiding, guiding. What remains
unless the dark heart fills new veins,
unless the creature slips her style?

## *Playing Dionysos in the* Bacchae

I moved him, and he moved in me by power,
knowing the pulse and the refrain of blood
that pumped a spring into the veins of dance
along the water's edge and in its hour.
The rhythm in a sparrow and a bud
left everything to art, to art and chance.

## Go Loudly, Pentheus

(Dionysos speaks)
Behind the time when dogwood starts to flower
I work and dance inside long changing days
to find the taste, the marrow of the hour
and twist it like a snake into a phrase
that stings with all the passion of a kiss
and smiles with anger in a lying mask
behind your back and turning in your wrist:
I give you back in blood the thing you ask.

And while you climb the mountain like a child,
expecting pleasures and a pretty dance,
I'll screw your trouble into a spring wild
and deadly in the hidden trap of chance.
Under your well-laid palace stones I've cracked
and wriggled like a rooting lightning-gale
and gently, sweetly in bright birds of fact
I'll wind fat songs of fancy up your trail.

Go loudly, grin behind your mask as dead
as I will make you in a ringing glade.
I take joy in the sour blood I've said
into your ignorant ears. Now fade
and take my phosphor in your vein
as suddenly as it has ripped your sky.
Hear as you die the innocent refrain
of birds inside your blue unseeing eye.

## Phaeton

I must explore this country of the dawn,
break purple into roses, let the fading stars
collapse beneath my wheels as I come on;
I must, I must discover at the end
my father's love, and bend those golden bars
as wisely as he does; I must suspend

the day in my careening metaphor
and feel the wind of power in my face,
discover after in what comes before.
These Hours and their moments must give way
to me, and in the motion of my grace
must open to me secrets of the day.

O father, give me time, yet give me speed.

Remembering, as I fall slowly, burn,
the morning full of roses and my need
I open to my own dawn and too late
enter the world I ruin to return
the quiet vengeance of my twisted fate.

My sisters drop their slow stone tears into
the river I speak from. Let your hand
drift lifeless in this water and look through
the myth of me. Out of these poplar trees
a young wind shakes like stars into the sand
those ambers: who hears, who in the current sees?

## Echo and Narcissus

What Echo could Narcissus find
as he flipped backward through his mind?
What femininity was there
developing behind his stare,
reflective face and sometime flower:
what Echo in that endless hour?

And she, hung in the woods, a voice
of atrophy, a futile choice,
devoted to her male ideal:
did she believe that he was real?
No doubt discovery and chase
lead to a story's light and grace:

a poet translates what remains,
and gives a haunting flower brains,
imagining his lover's cry
unheard to echo. No reply
lifts from the myth. The handsome boy
died faithful to his selfish joy.

## Translating Sappho

The breeze, so gentle to the sky,
has washed the page in shadow,
made the waking seem to find
their ghosts in growing form.

Upon the desk the left hand waits,
while this one hunches on the coming line
to call a ripple from its resting,
waiting echo and attempt

to turn the wave to coral.
It seems to have in tow
the dried anthea of the lady
Sappho, which in their

tender bearing come to bring
the touch of her hand strength
in mine: a pulse so deep
that hands are charmed.
Waking Sappho joins the dance.

## Glimpses

Glimpsed passingly,
                    the windows
lit
    with day's last images
                    involved
immediately
            an old dame,
                who took them in
as pictures
            stitched (maybe)
                    on her quilt
of quilts
           (a magic thing spread
snowy on her empty bed,
                  patched
crazy with bright flowers),
                  where
she would return.
                 Her raking muscles
stretched and dinner
                (an affair with dogs)
devising her to
           rest:
why die when sleep's so
                 good and
ghostly
         if you come to know
its pictures
            wrinkled but still clear,
the windows
            turning inward then.

## Shakespeare's Flowers*

Memory of flowers, filling up the face
that drifts reflective in its sense and speech,
the thought remembers him and in its grace
recalls the daisies of reflection, each
starred, blooming, a pupil in a learning eye
that shifts, diminishes and grows
from night to day, vanishing, returning,
becoming quince, harebell or rose
according to the mood of one who thinks
them from the ground like secret sounds
unheard exploding: yellows, purples, pinks
and deep blues; and the silence that surrounds
their growing smells sweet and forgotten, pressed
with the blossoms in their story, in their nest.


*After an arrangement of pressed flowers mentioned in
Shakespeare's works, by Barbara Whatmore.

## Séance

There was a certain pastness to the place
as if a resurrected memory
stopped silent in a photograph's embrace.
A dove in a moth-eaten maple tree
recalled a remnant image of croquet,
a séance of old empty chairs that spoke
without words all there ever was to say.
But why did I feel guilty as I broke
the gathering of spirits on the lawn
and later found again in candle light
the flickering picture where their sense hung on,
a little day that blossomed out of night
to open a schoolmistress and her mind?
The ghosts had left their medium behind.

## Chiaroscuro*

The trees that print so clearly blur
below in the round fountain's face
that wimpling slightly seems to stir
its image with the depth of slow
reflection and refraction, place
in tremor chiaroscuro

so lightly come to shadow's thought
as if within a Roman brain
its silence had been darkly sought,
this garden long developed green
to shift in silver its quick stain.
An empty park becomes the scene

translated by the shutter's choice
to memory. Misting the plate,
a meditative breath in voice
interprets fountain, trees and sky
to take a moment's life and weight
in balance, answering the eye.


*After a photographic *View of St. Peter's from the Pincian
Hill* by Robert MacPherson.

## Changeling

The sound track of the movie is a child:
voice of a shadow, sound of what we see,
it plays along the highways of our veins,
interpreting the image in the wild
old road map of its mystery. And we
following after through the woven lanes
watch the picture swallowing its dwindling light
as dark woods grow darker on the roadside page
and a story flutters down like a lure
into the expectancy of the night.
Thoughtless, the dancing image is engaged
and steps into the flickering moment sure
that it may shift until the last light dies.
The shadow is the child, the voice is wise.

## The Innocents

Innocent in thunder, four
faces in a photograph
behind the camera's door
against a painted storm, half

smile into the mirror lens
and gather darkly like a cloud
within the little sky of friends.
Their eyes and hands are proud

to make the picture real
and, helpless as they are,
to feel
what impulse left the door ajar.

## Surprise

In the midst of your word the snapshot fell,
a black and white translation. Here it was
almost April, nineteen forty-three—spell
of cool spring. The spider shadows pause
on the porch. It seems to be afternoon.
No telling why your daughter came so soon.

## What Happens Happens

What happens happens by the purest chance,
a spring from winter out of summer's fall,
the only dancer in the only dance

who breathes the shades of passage and enchants
the little bigness of the hugely small.
What happens happens by the purest chance,

cutting in the angles a diamond slants,
this gem, the shifting character of all,
the only dancer in the only dance.

In the sure uncertainty of advance
the present is a wedding of may and shall.
What happens happens by the purest chance.

A sensing animal can quickly glance
inside; understand, forget, recall
the only dancer in the only dance

whose open secret moves in conscious trance
in the full quiet of an empty hall.
What happens happens by the purest chance,
the only dancer in the only dance.

# Restoration

*For Phyllis Mount*

In a remembered gallery of scenes
where figures faded or revived under
the restorer's brush, I saw my mother
wander through the rooms as if her tense
had changed, as if our minds were ruined
gardens and the windows' wimpled lights looked out
upon their fountains crumbling in doubt.
The rubblestone of sculpted myths thinned

suddenly away. The framed glass melted
into a morning landscape that had been
our own, where trees ballooned and hovered
in the wind that swayed the meadows belted
by old roads that led through towns, that began
somewhere and reached for countries undiscovered.

## First Redstart

He handed me two trembling coins of glass
enveloping the image of a flame
trapped in a bird that flickered as it came
into the centre that it held at last.

## Bulbs

A world so close to sleep
is saved by motion
and bulb stirrings deep

enough under the skin,
down almost forgotten
among their clustering kin,

workings in black dirt
pushing up the stem
a spurt

we recognize as flower.
The deaf-mutes rise
inside the hour

where their leaves belong
and carve its light with green.
Not one will pull the wrong

blossom from the fist
cogitating,
spinning out, without a twist,

its date
from memory that shows
before too late.

# Hydrangeas

## 1

Wicked midwinter:
tattered hydrangeas
still sprout a mean
blossom, brown
against new snow.

Twice-told the simple
mirror makes them
and from all angles
they blow purpose
into the air
like whales; or are they
pulmonary angels?

Something angelic, yes.
Taking me seriously,
they hang translated.

## 2

Look underneath
at the flower ceilings
fed through light struts
into silent frame.
What an extravagance,
what a glory,
thought through the world
like a palmist's register
instant, constant,
perfect, pure.

## 3

Let us not burn
them. They have enough
flame already.
Lit with their shape
they rise fiery
like a blue
moment captured
fiercely. Let us just
watch them
incandesce
until they whisper
in crows' voices
afternoon's end
and the night's waking.

## Locusts

I love the twist
in those dark trees,
the curve that from the stone wall
winds in multiple and
elegant duress made easy
by the swing, the effortlessness
of the windy words
they are, strung handsomely
across the field like
soldiers at their haughty ease,
cheeks wrung and arms
extravagant . . . .

## Barn Morning

*For Richard Bliss*

Getting toward six-thirty when the sun
shoves light through chinks to stripe the old barn red
inside     like a huge lantern whose beams run
the length of the great wooden beams     light shed
holding the weight of hay and long dark wings
on rafters     We stretched up into the mow
to find bats birds and holes of sky where things
spoke in the dusky lift of then     not now

And thumping down with hay for horse and sheep
out to the barnyard past the milkers cold
as fingers squirting in a second sleep
with Milly's foot in bucket as the morning     gold
now     wrapped the rustling hay in smoky light
scattered to outside animals along
the cold ramainder of the wind and night
We stump back     swing the door     and risk a song

Then to the chickens mad and cannibal
upstairs we steal their eggs     warm under breasts
along the galleries of a cackling wall
and stealthily     their treacherous quick guests
we filch ourselves down their stiff creeping stairs
into the horse stable with black tack hung
and sounding thunder     as geldings and mares
stop     to present their still ghosts to be sung

Dennis     most ghostlike in his cloud of weight
by Sybil brown and black-maned in her steam
who dragged us down on homemade sled to skate
Frog Hollow     in the icy dusky scheme
returning     Ward at the reins and Betsy's bells
tingling in the blue coming-on of night
I found a horse whose quiet story tells
as simply as her colour on deep white

But come back to the barn      and hear the end
the milkers gathering their pails      the hog
grunt      settling down into new straw      Descend
for a last look into the yard      the dog
aimless happy in his untroubled day
trotting among slow sheep that cluster in the snow
and watch in innocence behind the gray
barn      the last of their old masters      go

## Incursion

The shy doves wheeled and scattered creaking gray
out of the cranky apples and in flocks
of three or four displaced settled to stay
in higher branches when, snow in my socks,
toting my saw, I walked into their world
and took their place. The slow saw popped and chewed
and blurring round the bar as the chain curled
the birds slipped in my branches, blew my mood
with light. And I held them in my head
to shift and gather, flutter like the words
they were by now. The long shiver I said
came out of beating wings those quiet birds
made ruffle through my eyes into my tongue
where shuddering they could be darkly sung.

## What Someone Sings

Such swerves and slivers of last light
as flash in opening the cove
to its own darkness, looping, bite;
as fit the finger to the glove

and slip in silver what must turn
black, unremembered: these are lives
finned coldly yet awake to burn.
Inevitably night arrives:

the streetlight lays its silent beam
across the water, and the rings
lock into one another's gleam,
imagining what someone sings.

## Looking East

The culture of a seacoast, sand,
smashed shells, the thighbone of a bird:
the water foams and in the froth
big bubbles weakly pop.
                              I heard
an echo's Agamemnon die;
in his impassive golden mask
see spread the arrogance of kings
as it collects a few last things
to carry if it could, defy
the summons of the earth and sky.

Beyond the ritual of death
only another gathered breath
fills a new body and becomes
a character who cannot know
what happened in the darkness when,
buried in ancient lives, old men
engraved their images in gold.
So many stories go untold.

## Manhattan

Down in a green remainder
among climbing stones,
where gulls crumple and soar,
where a steel bridge breathes people
into the glowing town:

the mind wanders
in its own deep streets,
pauses and repeats old conversations
that lean from dark windows,
familiar, unwrinkled,
in the noise of horns.
A window ledge
suddenly is undone with leaves.
A rambling breeze
crumbles the building
to a tree. Follow its roots
to the river, where the last boat
of the Circle Line
passes toward its disappearing slip
in a hazy harbour
that is turning (slowly)
green.

## Settling In

### 1

At first the place seems somewhat strange.
The princess and the prince are here
to make a mockery of change;
suspended by their strings, appear
to take no notice of the time,
only of one another, blond:
silent, from embroidered eyes, they mime
devotion. But you move beyond
that stillness into what is new.
Yet even that seems old. You come
to find an early part of you.
And something in this medium,
this friend in whom your pasts converge
is finding her way home again
to nest in your uncertain urge
to welcome her, to be her friend.


### 2

This phoebe, watchful from her nest—
a cup, a corner, grass and mud—
comes quietly as you, to rest,
and in the impulse of your blood
*is* strange. She stirs you with her wings
and thump, the measure of her heart.
Once in a while, through you, she sings:
this wonder is the song you start
in building your house around her,
in taking her to be your muse.
She's nothing that is all you choose.
She loves you, but at first afraid
flies from your footstep and the bang
of the screen door. What has she made?
Was it her breath or yours that rang?

3

Again in the old window glass
a man walks toward you, stops to look
as you do. Such reflections pass
into your life, into your book:
you cannot stop them, and you feel
at home with that exact response.
This place will never be less real
for having dreamed you. You ensconce
that being that your image greets
on the front porch, and let it write.
The nature that your phoebe meets
is all-inclusive. In that light
you open up not just this place
but every cabinet you own;
and birds fly out. In your new face
you see your self. You are alone.


4

In the flat stones out front you find
a history: drawn up by ox,
they were laid in your memory
to carry you into your mind:
the rings that maple stump unlocks,
remembering its winters. See,
the trunk lies heavy on the ground,
shot with concrete, defying saws.
The tree is rotting slowly but
once stood with others in the sound
you hear, wind through new leaves. You pause
to listen to the evening cut
in under birdsong, under bloom.
You find again your dusky room.

## Stay Here

The corn now marching weary
                                    still:
detachments
                    in dead gardens
wilt,
        a silo
                sags. This tired old country
slows me
            down.
                        A woman
                                    hanging
on a cigarette
                    speaks through teeth
to a spotted dog:
                    'Stay here,
stay
        here.'

## Dunbarton's Dreams

*In Memoriam, Robert Lowell*

The sun is melting caves in sky and land
and in them fall the bones of men. Men's graves
climb hills and sag in valleys, silver waves
or copper brown, whispering in sand.

The snow sifts into the ground of April,
dying snow, whose disappearance means the end
of that blank season where we freeze. We mend
our ears with birdsong and a growing will.

Dying is perhaps a change, a knocking
of the frame that shifts the picture ever
so slightly, and brings what once was never
ever so slightly nearer, clear, unlocking.

## Birds of Light

*In Memoriam,*
*Harry Greenwood Grover*

The riddled brass lantern
sees its own light fly.
The old man's birds of light
from the shadow side of morning
wake in a spooky flock
that waves in the dangle of the day.
The gulls keep their lift
silent in the sober room
and only the footsteps of the clock
rush forward to the signal chime.

## Parson Ashley

The frogs weird in the arbour shade
remember Parson Ashley's trance,
by heaven and the haps of chance
the world of words he must have made
out of the shadows' blinking glade,
a puritanical romance
of nature and the need to dance:
how else pick up the parson's trade?

Here hellishly where dark met light
surrender was an act of faith:
in later years he joined his wife
in absolution's second sight;
the tremor of wraith dark in wraith,
a birds' nest in the eaves: his life.

## Intimates

He felt the small of her back smooth
and rubbed it slightly with his palm
as if a gentle mind could soothe
through that wimpled plateau of bone
into the depth she held alone.
He felt a curious dark calm:

perhaps her depth slept in his hand,
a shadow darkening the time
that beat there where he'd understand
and take her message like a breath,
presentiment of life past death,
the turn, the everlasting rhyme.

She woke then. He could feel her sleep
slip and vanish, and her wake
fill him with more than he could keep.
He saw it surely in her eyes
and in the moment of surprise
considered whether he could break

the silence with a deeper word
from which slow rippling rings would grow.
Not listening, she must have heard;
turned to him with a simple grace
and wondering explored his face
and said like a mist, I know you know.

## One on One

I catch myself
        at work on
                me
and stop it.
        Self,
           I say,
be lesser than
your silent
        friend,
           the moth
who purple
        hovers here
                drying
her laundry
        on your
             line,
from pin to pin an anxious
                soul
who stretches you.
           And be more
droll.

## Each in Each

Nineteen, the geese reflected here
in stitches by the mirror twice
across a blue sky and a wood
of fantastic flowers. Queer,
as if at the shake of some dice,
some cosmic dice, I chance in good
to find, upon a dresser, fall,
and summer on the other wall.

The night is wobbling along
a passage caught in this old word,
recalcitrant as badgers, tough
to tumble into life in song.
The hour-glass around the bird
waits for its heartbeat: that's enough
to quiver on the edge of sight,
to be the creature of this night,

who is a magic acrobat.
Who lingers on the tongue of time
and jumps like fury into dark
and disillusion; is a cat

bound to the dangle of this rhyme.
Who turns to look, and stops to bark,
its protean unshape a dream
exciting to behold, redeem

into wherever you are now.
Wherever we are, you and I
who make together like the glass
reflections of a world, of how
we find in silence and the sky,
among the flowers, in the grass,
the thought, the word, the reason in
the ages of the planet's spin.

How did we come to know the night?
We wondered, didn't we, and risked
a shadow for a sight of star.
We pondered in the quiet light
an animal who rose and whisked
away our every inward bar
and gave us all it could to teach
what love is, why each is in each.

## The Wizard's Question

Eh bravo! Here's morning.
Caught me
nodding
over my simples like
an old man,
            as I am.

What was I saying to me when?

Forget, forget.

Remember morning in
a bird's eye singing?

Take this, you'll remember.

See?

## Jazz

The crickets' rhythm,
same as mine,
impulsive as they find their tune.
They've got a beat
and down the whitewashed night
they dig the moon.

A candle in my eye reflects
like fireworks
the cricket stars
who sing unheard
around me. The reason
of this gab? Unknown
and rocking.
Scoop
the night into your jazz
and grow.

## Reflection

A double picture: in the glass
the present, and behind, still flowers.
Motion: that's the picture fast
changing as I lift my head
into its spell of leaves in red
motion, yes, commotion. Hours

of creation rest. In that shine
so much presented, passed, given.
Reflected, caught in such design,
time looks like a maple tree
delivered redly, leafed to me
in bequest, and I am riven:

twice the image I can frame
spins me, and I split. But still
black behind blooms bright the same
contemplation of the slow
creature I must come to know:
friend before friends, god whose will

opens this parade of light
and frees me to look up and find
all the silence due to sight.
The rush of wind faint in my ears,
the holy ghost of what appears,
is only part of what's behind

this revelation doubly true,
this subtlety, this manifold
and manifest ecstatic clue
to depth, to time, to all that's real
that poetry can see and feel,
the beauty we can never hold

except in pictures. Soul of art,
I speak to you, I touch your heart.

## When

When courage comes to sleep
in dusk, in bird; and night
subverts the seer's light
into a sky of steep

stars in a masque of fate
the constellations must
admit him to their dust.
Forgetting his own weight

he must remember how
to picture and to spin
the old worlds, to begin
in silence to allow

himself a sense of space;
if only darkness, then
a readiness for when.

## Winds

The winds are forgiving.
I work by just living.

The winds now are chilling.
I work by distilling.

The winds now are done.
I live by the sun.

## Turning

In the gray valley imagined,
fringe of a stirring forest
moves in the twilight thinking
birds with their muted voices.

Darker the night remembers,
coming to open stillness.
Where in the darkened forest
whisper the birds in hiding?

This is the time to listen.
Now in the turning branches
soft by the wind translated,
thoughts of night are nesting.

Colin Way Reid was born in Sweet Briar, Virginia, in 1952 and grew up in South Hadley, Massachusetts, where he took his own life at the age of thirty. He studied at East Hill School in Andover, Vermont, at St. John's College in Maryland, at the University of Virginia, at Mount Holyoke College where he took classes in classics and English, and at the University of Massachusetts in Amherst, where he took an A.B. degree in the University Without Walls.

Certain of these poems have appeared in *A Review* and in *Poetry Ireland*; 'Temenos', 'Changeling', 'The Innocents', and 'The Sleeping Gypsy' appeared in *The Sewanee Review*, Sewanee, Tennessee, and grateful acknowledgement is made to the editor, George Core, and the University of the South. 'Rembrandt's Tobit' won a Duncan Lawrie prize in the Sotheby's International Poetry Competition (London) of 1982 and appeared in the *Anthology* of that year. 'Manhattan' and 'After William Blake' have been set to music by Allen Bonde, and performed.

This selection of poems, written between 1977 and 1983, has been chosen and arranged by Colin's parents, Jane and Ben Reid.